LAYERS

LAYERS

E. R. Welch

authorHOUSE®

AuthorHouse™
1663 Liberty Drive
Bloomington, IN 47403
www.authorhouse.com
Phone: 1-800-839-8640

Published by AuthorHouse   01/13/2015

ISBN: 978-1-4918-0543-5 (sc)

To someone unforgettable
Our moments under sun and moon
To love and madness as a muse
And to the healing yet to come

CHAPTER 1
ANTHEM OF STING AND EMBER

Him

He made summer in to song
He put laughter in my life
He led me from my silent nights
And yet the sun has set again
The world, I know must always turn
Leaves of autumn fall once more
If only time was circular

Gone

Where is my love?
Where is my loss?
The mirror I give a careless glance reflects nothing

Where is my joy?
What is my name?
When I stand in the sun, where's my shadow?

Where is my fear?
Where is my hate?
The eyes gazing through me seem luminous

Where is my sorrow?
Where is my song?
Though I walk through the waters they remain still

Where is my laughter?
Where is my life?
When I scream in the night, where's the sound?

The music in my words is gone
The sparkle in my eyes once strong
Has been blown out as if a candle
But even on this I'd've gained handle
If you too hadn't disappeared
With all of my mind memory and tears

You my friend my dear one my only
In the end you glared at me stonely
And that last look to me revealed
All the thoughts you'd ever congealed
You didn't care at all about me
I was an object to observe and see
You found me amusing, that's why you stayed
And in your death you needed my aid
That is when you truly ceased
Not when you fell to the ground beneath
Not when that thing called a body died
Not as it lay crumpled on its side
Not as I wiped the blood off my face
Not as I dragged it up to the dais
I was still following your careful instruction
I gave the body your requested destruction
The fire burned hard, deep, and strong
It wasn't surprising it took me along

Emptiness

Through long live night I watched
While watched back I silently suffered
Staring at opaque life, wondering, pondering
If possibly I exist somehow beneath the words
Or around them, rather than within
Images with immense illumination surround
But I am not there, or anywhere
My presence is not its self, only emptiness
A dead star, absorbing all but full of nothing
A substance of nonsubstance beyond reach
A gaping hole in the fabric of matters
Devoid of its own self and that which we call space
So I am that which I am not
Perhaps a test on this plane
But in the very depth of it, only emptiness

Gone (continued)

Now I am nothing neither dead nor alive
I am something only you would contrive

Of course you brought me too
I always went with you
Death when we were so entwined
Resulted in this paradigm

Dark insanity
Is all that is left to me
Velvet never ending night
Eternally holds on tight

Touch me and I cannot feel
If this is sickness, let me heal
Existence devoid of all
Please be a dream withal

Yet some part of me is here
'Cause I sense that life is near
A shard of me must be alive
A single piece must have survived

Maybe one day the wind will blow
And make this tiny ember grow
But then my only, my dear one, my friend
I would wonder why did you end?

Where is your laughter?
Where is your frown?
Why is your bed made the way you never left it?

Where is your guidance?
Where is your face?
Only in the pictures packed away

Where is your dancing?
Where is your dawn?
I will miss the love that you never felt

Where is your singing?
Where is your soul?
Did you have one in the first place?

Where is your mischief?
Where are your plans?

Despite what you did
Had I not had you at all
I would have been dead long ago

Mindless Inquisition

I look
And all the colors
Begin to fall
Around me softly

It seems
That life is
Slowly, surely
Melting into rain

I watch
The blood of
Today and tomorrow
Pooling in the stones

Is it
Sad or beautiful
The death
Of all these things

Why do
All the people
From this
Seek to gain an answer

Why are
There minds
Hungry
For what they cannot find

They'll keep
Plowing onward
Relentless
Till they're dying

Throwing
Life away
To find the
Meaning of it

Mindless inquisition

Once Upon December

My one, my only
Careless beside me
Beautiful were you
If you'd been true

Oh so many people died
And yet I never cried
Didn't shed a single tear
All because of you my dear

Do you know what you did that day?
Threw my childhood away
Took my only firm foundation
Welcomed death as a vacation

I hid behind the door
You looked and I was it once more
So innocent
That's my lament

My one my only
Where did you hide from me?
That mind I know was yours?
That chamber of horrors?

My one my only
Wretched beside me
All alone with out a care
All alone though I was there

Serpent underneath
The flower that you seemed

Thoughtlessly terrible
Mindlessly evil

So psychotic
So hypnotic

My one, my only
Where did you hide from me?
That mind I know was yours?
That chamber of horrors?

My one my only
Wretched beside me
All alone with out a care
All alone though I was there

Mindless Inquisition (continued)

Is there
Meaning in a
Foot print on the sand
That washed away?

As dust
We are no
Different
Vanishing into night

Yet still
They keep on climbing
Keep on trying
To fill the void

Is
Everything we do
A means to
Lie about the question?

I must
Admit that this
Is something
I don't know

Mindless Inquisition

Patch Work Quilt

Stranger, stranger by my side
From you I cannot hide
In my eyes that's your reflection
Those twisted thoughts your resurrection

Lurking in a darkened truth
You watched quiet through my youth
Till the day when awoken
Then my solitude was broken

In nights where foot steps echo in my mind I cannot
breathe
Stranger restless stranger can't you wander off and
leave?

Ebony insanity
My companion this deep canyon
In reality

Do I know you better than I'd ever care to say?
Are you staring at me in the mirror every day?

Inside the web you've sown
While stronger you have grown
Lost in incubus unfolding
Is there a shred of truth upholding?

I cry out so desperately
Yet only you answer me
So much havoc inside one head
Life has become different shades of red

Ebony insanity
My companion this deep canyon
In reality

Song of Sadness

A million little things
Use to make my spirit sing
But now in this silent night
There are dreams but there is no light
Time and time again
I wish this shadow life would end
Why does every mind
Long for something it can't find?
Is there a question I could ask?
To lay these things to rest at last?
Time and time again
I wish this shadow life would end

Untitled

I lived for you, my angel and demon,
Through nights blacker than sin it's self
I breathed for you, kindest and cruelest,
Though pain was almost all I knew
I laughed for you, my lovely and terrible
Sang for you, danced for you,
Cut for you, bled for you
Was your life so hopeless you had to take it?
From me?
What happened to the patience that you taught?
Could it have waited one more day?
For a time when my identity
Wasn't tied to yours the way it was?
No.
You had a careful plan
Had to jump when you did
That silhouette against the sky
Changed me into what I am
I knew it then
I know it now
Still I am ever wondering why
Couldn't you have lived for me?
The way I did for you those years?

Goodbye

Feather I must let you go
For too many lives I've held on tight
Carried you through sun and storm
Watching time fly over head
But the spider spins his web again
New mountains rise from the sea
The trickling spring finds renewal
You and I were just a dream
So I'm casting you away
Float on the brightened breeze
Visit me no more my feather
I release you here at last
Time to pick up scattered pieces
You left lying on the floor
Time to seek another puzzle
As this one will not be solved
You took too many pieces with you
The last time you tried to fly
Goodbye single feather
The time has come
And again I say goodbye

CHAPTER TWO
EXCERPTS FROM 2002-2006

Wisdom

Life is nothing but a song
A smile, a laugh, a sigh
Take a walk through waters long
And fear, despair, and cry
Pace upon the third stone
Drink a cup of love
Knowing how the birds have flown
We think of things above
Thoughts are but a rock
That skims an effervescent pool
And what a marvelous shock
When we sink beneath the schools
Of the fish swimming 'round
Scales all agleam
Then we will know what's sound
And what can only seem

Look

In a dream I dreamt one night
I saw the crescent moon alight
On red roses on the snow
On the darkness down below
The streams of water song
The tide of life that ebbs along
The path ways to the ocean
Swept forward in this constant motion
And with every wave that breaks
With every scream a child makes
There are echoes everywhere
In the water and in the air
And if one decides to listen
In their eyes tears will glisten
So in this state of sadness
Some close their ears missing the gladness
At their finger tips
The truth that is on the lips
Of someone that they've ignored
All their lives, of their own accord
Therefore keep your mind open
For whosoever can know when
Light and wisdom will bloom above
And explain to us the mysteries of love

Truth

Softly velvet keys arranged
Like stair steps rising, though estranged
To night they travel onward
And to light the path a songbird
Flying high and swift above
Across the moon while memories of
The labyrinth behind the three
Reveals to them the mystery
That they must face together
That will change their lives forever
There is a lesson they must learn
Cruelty will take its turn
Beauty lies within destruction
Love, hate, fear, and corruption
Have their times, as do we all
Every person hears a call
And with whatever words they answer
May determine, but hope a dancer
In the hearts and minds of men
A burning ember pray thee then
Share with others this tiny spark
To keep it burning against the dark

Our Story

In the night I am alone
With memories not my own
Starlight and silver snow
Pale winter moon aglow
Mirrored in your brilliant eyes
So with this interlude I rise
To find the world a music note
In a song that someone wrote
Melodies of divine design
As the planets all align
A destiny unique to me
Reveals itself on stormy seas
After the tempests final fire
After those with one desire
Have perished in a single clash
Then vanished in a cloud of ash
Petals of the rose will scatter
But in the dark it will not matter
Remember what I used to say
You and I will fly someday

Untitled

Sunset sunrise life
Always ending and beginning
Circular and effervescent
This universe where
Death is life's renewal
Silently each cycle
Like the phases of the moon
Play out divine plans.
What will my destruction create?

Beautiful

Contained in circles of fire and ice
Of liquid embers immersed in night
Within pinpoints of infinite depth and darkness
Lies wildness that cannot be harnessed
Twin pools, two windows, into your life
Cut into a velvet sky with a knife
Framed by cascades of crimson and gold
Filled with stories never been told
A whirlwind of hair, an intense winter face
Eyes streaked with fire, and nonchalant grace

Why?

The mind, a restless tool, carelessly tossed
On a shelf, hidden, hopelessly lost
As the summer drains away
Sleep has taken night and day
How much longer will it take?
From your slumber to awake?
Wasting the gifts under the sun
Wasting, wasting, are you ever done?

A Death

It's silent now
The night has come
The laughter's gone
And I'm alone

Snow flakes fall
Cleansing the earth
A killing frost
Flowers are dying

The moon hangs
Deep in the sky
Cold and lidless
Silver in essence

Sakura falls
Just like the snow
Over and over
Like waves in my head

Once there were smiles
Once there were two
Though night is beautiful
There is no one to share it

Tragedy Repaired

Pictures scattered on the floor
Memories of thoughts no more
Innocence and a life shattered
No one thought it even mattered
A dark seedling took its hold
A dark meaning did unfold
Inside the eyes and mind
Of one by nature kind
But beside a broken truth
Looking back on tainted youth
The child becomes a demon
No one looked for the reason
Not one cared to share his pain
On himself he placed the blame
Lost in deepened devastation

Striving towards alienation
Till at last a little girl
Saw fit to invade this world
She made him recall who he was
He stopped hurting all because
Of simple uncomplicated love
Very much a gift from above
Though his horrors were never forgotten
From them new joys were begotten
So he lived out a life
Not totally devoid of strife
But neither was it missing pleasure
And he regards it as a treasure

A Mind Less Than Whole

Puzzle with pieces missing
Dances alone in the city of rain
The sad song she is singing
Is filled with otherworldly pain
Haunting and lyrical,
Beautiful and intricate,
It seems to be a miracle
That a song should have such life in it
Underneath the cherry tree
Petals fall in Puzzle's hair
She sings for you and me
With flowers falling everywhere
Between two worlds she walks the line
One is light the other dark
Back and forth all the time
In the ship she calls her ark
Seconds are like grains of sand
But they're turning into years
Decades slip through her hand
While the sky never clears
Still she is alone and friendless
In solitude she loves and hates
Her life is seeming all too endless
She can't wait till she escapes

Not With Out a Witness

My essence must be sadness
Sorrow is my simple song
Despair my melody
But the world is full
Of saddened dreamers
God, He sees each tear
That is what makes them matter

Ode to *Lord of the Flies*

Children sing of nothing, nothing
Children sing and fall away
Softly, softly voices mixing
Softly, softly all the day
Whispering they move the earth
Chanting cracks the drying ground
Their feet align but no one's first
Turning, turning all around
Children sing of never, never
Children sing and break away
Softly, softly faces mixing
Softly, softly every day
They vanish two into silence
Vanish in the ocean's tide
In an act of practiced violence
Gave them to the lord of flies

Not in Sight

A breath can change a life
The prick of a needle
A bump on the head
Anything can alter everything
Maybe there is no fate
Only cause and effect
All actions are preceded by others
As they are followed by more
Is there an end?
A conclusion?
Is there a finishing point?
To the results?
Do the things I have done evaporate
When I am gone?
If they did,
If the past ceased with the arrival of the future
Then there would be no causality
Nothing could make anything different
Actions would be pointless
Meaningless

I and the person I was five minutes ago
Exist together
My past shapes my now
In that sense my past is my now
Every second merges with the next
They become one
Every event becomes larger
It expands
Combining and multiplying
Stretching out like the branches of a tree
These paths overlap
If one tosses a pebble into a pond
The ripples add to each other
They become new things
Reactions always lead to another
There was a beginning
But an ending?
Never.

The Root of Things

Crimson tide beneath my skin
Treasure that is found within
Moving through the finger tips
Flowing under scarlet lips
Below what we see and touch
Yet the sight I love so much
Here in is light and darkness
Deeper life, our farthest farness
The living and the dead's protection
The divine intervention
Beautiful and terrible
Simply incomparable
This gateway to another world
A declaration, a flag unfurled
Bigger than us and yet smaller
Shorter than us and much taller
The flaming light of eternity
I long for in adversity
Fall on the city of rain
Fall only to fall again

A New Chapter in Alone

It eats away, some sore of soul
A cancer of the heart
Some virus of the higher mind
So small at the start
I know the demon and the pain
I know the horrid view
Of the years I'll spend by myself
A bird reminds me too
Alone like Edgar Allen Poe
In solitary thought
Alone like David Berkowitz
Though killer I am not
So sing to me a love song, silence
That I might love you back
Maybe then my happiness won't rest
On everything I lack

CHAPTER 3
ROMANCE

The Words

Beautiful words
Spoken to me
That soft silence
Lingered
In the core
Of my being

Beautiful eyes
The innocence found
In their depths
Is so sincere
And so honest
That it hurts me

Beautiful lips
Pressed against mine
In this special
Moment
I won't soon
Forget

Beautiful hand
That rests in my own
That has
Since we began
Our walk
In the snow

Beautiful body
Warm in the cold
On this starry night
As I wonder
Could this person
Exist?

Beautiful soul
That I can't
See or touch
But I know that its there
Because you
Are alive

Beautiful tongue
That spoke me
The words
I smile as
I tell you
That I love you too

Untitled

I know of the forbidden fruit
The heart is where its tree takes root
Perhaps you are reflected in it
Is this woven in mind's spinet?
You, a taste on wind, of it
Those nearer to the storm I covet
Kiss me with your mouth of rain
That grows the sweetening sugar cane
Embrace me with the sound of thunder
Though my soul is torn asunder
The clouds your grey-green eyes of mist
They always make my judgment twist
I want to love you always, ever
But perhaps this is a trap so clever
Yet hold me tight a little more
Though not solid at the core
You are the tempest and a treasure
Perhaps a test or a measure
Yet you bring me mostly grief
You caused my soul to strike a reef
Sing to me, oh baneful match
Put back the other hearts you catch
Am I the forbidden one to you?
I deeply hope this isn't true

The Return

He came to me like winter roses
Or a zephyr on the snow
As the sun comes out of hiding
And the dawning day takes hold
So he crept over the mountains
Setting all the clouds aflame
With colors bright and transcendental
Like the promise in the rain
There was no song; there was no silence
No huzzahs, no trumpet sound
But in my heart such grand elation
For at last my love was found

A Physics Love Song

You are the harmony
Of the infinitesimal
The simple complexity
Of the quantum
You are the balance
Of the strong
And the weak force
Plus the bending of these
Rules that make the sun
You are the Euclidian
Geometry of space
As well as the motes
And liquids of time
The event horizon
Is like you
A gateway to questions

And perhaps the answers
To questions we don't know
But most of all,
You are like love
A strange force
Sometimes counterintuitive
Powerful and awesome
That's of God
And is God
He gives it to us
As He gave me you
And you are like it
As you are like this cosmos
The two meet in you

Untitled

My earth-heaven, my only, my lost one, friend
My songbird, my firestorm, my beginning, end
I always thought grey a lifeless color
But in your eyes it is something other
It is the silver-metallic edge of a knife
It is somberly sad, yet impossibly blithe
It is the grey of stones under clear mountain streams
The grey of living shadows at midnight's dreams
Behind those eyes lay my redemption
Almost constantly I ask the question
"Why did you save me at all?"
"How could you hear my silent call?"
"When even I was in ignorance to it?"
I'll ask it again,
"Why did you do it?"
I don't understand your labyrinth mind
It must be the strangest man can find
Such a beautiful mind, such wondrous eyes
Yet the wild and terrible are also comprised
Inside with tragedy and madness
Still I am filled with great gladness
Whenever I see you beloved, friend
Lost one, firestorm, songbird, end

Chapter 4

DEAR SCHIZOPHRENIA,

Dear Schizophrenia,

You are the cornerstone of fear
The Raven of my mind
That dark and terrifying bird
Darting in and out of time
You are the monster and its maker
You are the voices in the night
You're a lover and a hater
Hidden deep inside
We are bound by double helix chains
Tyrants unto themselves
The iron fist of DNA
Encoded in my cells
You are a meaning I can't fix upon
A lesson I can't learn
The place at which I turned wrong
A darkness that can burn
You're the sense of ever being alone
A lack of perceived connection
But you are the ripple, I am the stone
And one day I'll be your correction

Dear Schizophrenia,

    In poisoned silence, while laughing inward,
This Moment, made from hollow husks of time,
Comes crashing down, like waves upon her,
Catching on her opened soul.
Wind weaves words into her conscious,
The wailing of the walking storm,
Anchored deep inside the withermind,
Into which the grasping winter stole.
The world, now frozen, over and over,
Grins, encased again in blood of time.
As these crystaled points keep pasts alive.
So shall sanity be kept, as memory,
As light from stars, that shine on earth,
Though they are dead in their sky.

Dear More than Schizophrenia,

The wind whispers my name
A mighty vault of night
Echoes syllables in silence
Beyond and through
The birth of time
Words are a magic
And a channel in my universe
Shadowing my thoughts
As a chasm or a star that burst
In a world that was wreathed in quiet
Sound does not have a place
So these planes must be torn apart
And entered in another way
I see my mind
Now written backward
In the mirror that senses touch
In my ears the skies are screaming
Because the knife is very dull
Healing is a slow process
All of nature seeks to find
I know that outside this break
I will find a fate that's far more kind

CHAPTER 5
EXCERPTS FROM 2007-2010

The Cat Fights Back
(Schrodinger's Cat)

The Man:

I do not see it
Am not with it
Cannot measure
Cannot hear

Observation
No description
That must mean
It is not there

The box is true
The box is real
But the cat inside
I cannot feel

I am aware
I have thought
But what I do not sense
Does not

The Unusually Intelligent Cat:

I do not see him
Am not with him
For all I know
He may be dead

Though I'm the one
Trapped here with poison
What about
Reverse effect?

He can't see
He can't tell
But I can think
I might as well—

Decide myself
Who is alive,
Or does his thought
Count more than mine?

Can this man make-
Me live or die?
When *I* know-
My circumstances?

I'll thought kill him
Or at least try
So *my* mind
Can take its chances

Turning

Memories of shattered glass
Lost words and thoughts that lash
Add a broken injured mind
Yet the only joys I can find
Lie in those thoughts as well
Though they toll inside me like a bell
Like a time bomb, tick, tick, tick
Like a candle losing wick
My mind unravels like a thread
While my body thinks its dead
While it slumbers and acts the part
Except for my beating heart
I'm trapped in memories and thought
And the feeling these have wrought
Upon my frail being
When the same things I am seeing
I choose to visit thought or past
I'll always recall that shattered glass
As the tangent my life took
If I'd read it in a book

I'd know it was a hinging moment
That caught me up like a torrent
In my soul and layers deeper
I know there are few mountains steeper
Than the one I must climb now
I am ever wondering how
How do I ascend this body cage
How to put aside silent rage
How to reconcile years of pain
To once again be somewhat sane?
I don't know how, I don't know why
But I won't let life pass me by

Genius

The mind is eccentric
The matter is grey
The mind is electric
It's always at play
With ideas looked over
Ideas ignored
And impossibility rover
Because it is bored
With convention
Such things are so dull
Original invention
Are the thoughts that roll
In this mind
Where rules are suspended
Look in it and find
That all is upended
All things can be done
It says to itself
Infinity plus one
Solutions on the shelf
More neural connections
Make thought life a breeze
But people directions
Can be something one needs

An Old Tale

And there it were. In shadow it lay, awaiting its next victim.
We drew our swords, with battle cry, shouting the name of the
kingdom.
We must have been a sight to see, the hundreds marching forward.
But even more so was the beast as we struggled onward.
Fear easily grips the hearts of men. This time was no exception.
Though we came quite well prepared, we longed for more
protection.
Yet we forced it out, into the sun, where it reared and snarled.
In full fledged fight we engaged, between trees old and gnarled.
Metal was bent, banners torn, helmets smashed and broken.
And though there was horrific noise, very few words were spoken.
The monster lashed out with its tail, creating desolation.
When I saw that we might loose I called out in desperation.
"Do you remember?" I screamed at the nightmare. Its head
swiveled toward me.
It remarkably heard, for it loudly proclaimed, "I remember all
that I see!"
"You were very young, perhaps three or four, the day when we first
met."
"You've always escaped, that will change today. Don't let your
feeble mind fret."
Through the fright and fury, for its words may have well come
true,
But in that taught moment, my dear one, I saw you.

The "evil" laughed, for it knew my thoughts, and considered love a weakness.
I surveyed the damage, the bloodied ground, a scene of utter bleakness.
Then I expressed my mirth as well, filled with strange elation.
It came to this: a fearsome beast and a man who fought for his nation.
The others watched with gruesome awe as my armor split asunder.
The thing pleased with this provocation then made its fateful blunder.
So self assured, so confident, convinced of superiority,
I hadn't attacked, merely stood my ground my ground, looking as in some deformity.
It easily pushed aside my sword, but this was all part of my plan.
I ducked and rolled, picked up a stone, and when the time was right I ran.
With ferocious roar of victory, it began instinctive chase.
The hope of those depending on me failed with my haste.
I led it far, I led it fast, I prayed it wouldn't fly.
For if it did the plan would fail and I would surely die.
At last! To the river I came, and to the waterfall.
Here in the final stage of the plot, I had to risk it all.
I jumped clear, swam to shore, alive but all alone.
And at this time I saw fit to take out my little stone.
When the beast showed its ugly head, I ripped off my sleeve,

Inserted the stone, spun it around, and flying let it leave.
The stone flew true, hard, and high.
It struck the beast upon the eye.
As the piercing cry of pain rang out, nearly deafening.
Now after all the fight and pain, there would come a reckoning.
The others cheered in ecstasy; they surged forward to assist.
For at last this vicious tormentor was about to be vanquished.
When they had it helpless, they gave me back my sword.
They pushed and drug me 'cross the ground, motioning forward.
I stood before the beast again, this time our roles reversed.
Yet oddly, I stayed my hand, more killing seemed perverse.
I said, "I was very young, perhaps three or four, the day that we
first met."
"You've always escaped; that will change today, don't let your
feeble mind fret."
My sword came down. I beheld the sky,
As I put out its other eye.
This, it seemed was the thing to do.
They let it go. I came home to you.
I dream about it now and then.
This particular battle does not want to end.
Does it wonder why I left it alive?
Or consider why I let it survive?
The answer lies with something you told me.
Something my mind has since been holding.
"Everyone, everything will eventually pass."

"It may take a long time, or be quick as with grass."
"There will be no mercy, our bodies all fail."
"Life is strong, but also quite frail."
"This is something we know. So there's no reason to hurry."

The End

Winter Lesson

Snow falls upon a man
He holds out an open hand
Feels the spinning world beneath
His mind lets his soul unsheathe
He cries, though he knows not why
In his hand the snowflakes die
First he counts them, one by one
On and on he misses none
How far did this one fall?
A long way for a thing so small
Its journey ended in his palm
An Odyssey, a silent psalm
The ironic tears on his face
They will make snow some other place
This is not lost on him
But again he follows thought's whim
No identicallity,
Is that individuality?
Or are they all more of the same?
"What has been will be again"
It occurs to him as he quoth
That they are a bit of both
On that note, he calms inside
The snow is not his to guide—
Shape, or be scattering down
There is peace in the thoughts he's found

A Need to Protect

The scent of battle fades
As the passage grows longer
So many years between
Soon all will be forgotten
This is my lamentation
That of the soldier and historian
For the swords that clashed,
The blood that spilt,
The final cries of victory,
Will all loose their potency
At the lengthening of years
Listen to the past, oh children of men
Do not be lulled to sleep
By the languid times of peace
Instead you must remember
The fates of your fallen
Even now the shadows stir
And they do not forget

Untitled

I know your hate.
I know your blood.
I've seen the way it boils,
When you see my face
Or think my name.
The taste of my death
In your thoughts
Is pure sweetness.
The power, a drug
Of enchanting addiction.
You long for that moment.
Live for that moment.
Bury the pain
Beneath that desire.
Sutured your heart
With the dream
Of mine stopping.
And will I oblige
Your dark deadly wishes?
Then who will you blame?
Who can shoulder that fire?
Surely it would turn in on itself.
And I do not believe
Even you could withstand it.
With all your intensity.
And whirling graced wisdom.

The truth is, I love you.
I can't have you hurting.
So when the day comes
That I give what you're asking,
I must make sure,
You will be ok after.
One day you can kill me.
One day I'll give in.
Then I'll be at peace
But you will keep living.
I want you happy.
So be patient, my Sunrise.
Till you can handle
All that you require.
You're not as strong
As you think, quite yet.
I know you much better
Than any other.
And I will be here
At your side till the end
That you'll give.
Though I ask
That you'll spare me
Stray thoughts
Here and there.

Unbroken

Through the peeled flesh of time,
Rendered in a bitter flame,
Lies the indestructible,
In a past that will not change

Ineffable the moments' passing
When future becomes memory
Seconds slough off here and there,
Like old skins, shed for new

A gap that's growing ever wider
This fire burns but can't consume
And with this pain comes creation
Grasped by ineternal minds

Veins may run through yesterday
Through last year, into tomorrow,
But the stroke of the brush was final
Life all pours into the now

The ancient days, as if in amber
Are preserved like they were new
No travel any where or when
Can shape what is already done

A Song for a Lost Dreamer

Windmill wishes lost in time
She holds his hand
She grasps his mind
Dandelion dreams are flying
Mixed with whispers from the stream
Between the worlds she's gone to scrying
On places where the veil is thin

Currents catch at leaves and daydreams
In the laughter, she tastes salt
The sun has swallowed all the Bravelings
The story ends as she feared
A swollen star sets on his soul
In the eyes that always mirror
Bright but lost in the gold

Blue in azure is the thread
So hard to follow
As ancient dead
From the life from whence they sprung
Vanished now, she's on knifes edge
With the elemental tongues
The life is close as the loss

Hand in heart she walks the border
Because he is now far away
Does the world prefer chaos to order?
Can she bring either forth?
Is either life in reach worth saving?
Or should she both in mercy shorth?
And a fading quill leave off?

The questions ask with harsh bravado
Every second they spring a new
Drumming out a beat staccato
Demanding answers deeper, truer
Than death alone can hope to give
Briefly these thoughts walk through her
Becoming written on mind stone

Then a focus, once more shifting
Turns to ash upon his meaning
A mind that, was once drifting
Becoming anchored in a storm
The thoughts, the dreams, and even nightmares
Given strength, and given form
While far, but home, he smiles

Memories

Words spoken long ago
Return to me as seasons flow
Familiar faces blurred by time
Again made clear within my mind

Children play in our old haunts
The same needs and the same wants
Present in each and everyone
In all those beneath the sun

Taking hands we spun around
I recall so well the friendship found
In the brighter summer days
The rest of life seems shades of grays

Those precious weeks within the past
They were as years but quickly passed
I wonder where they all are now
What does this mystery enshroud?

Above the stars and far away
Beyond all the things that fade
We are still together there
With our favorite dreams to share

Seeing In

Today I see in song
In wandering harmonies
Twisting turning melodies
Intricate music
It changes suddenly
Iridescent
The wings of butterflies
Dancing in the sun

Today I see in silence
Soft quiescent moments
Slowly passing
Like drops of rain
In an ocean
As if I am
Painting white
On white paper

Today I see in love
In highlights of emotion
Pouring out like a fountain
Overflowing boundaries
Making all people
Seem like children
As a child
We love best

Today I see in half light
Everything in shadows
Hiding deeper darkness
In the grays
Thinking they are neutral
But they are undone
In this thought

Today I see in truth
All I find is translucent
Including me
How frightening
The equations of the soul
Every action creates
An equal and opposing reaction

Last, I see in time
All things fade
Breakers turn stone to sand
Fire converts to ash
Then these things
Are blown away

Decision

Chapter one had just begun
While I went on skipping stones
Paying vague attention to
The language of the wind and time

The cacophony inside of me
Rose once more to purge the world
Ending summer where it stood
Drowning all my thoughts of life

The book I lost in loathsome frost
As I went tumbling in the dark
The worlds between me and the truth
All screaming out my name

There was a path through the wrath
Of the minds that gathered pointing
Licking lips while sucking marrow
Making hollowness of others' souls

Once, path discovered, I recovered
To find the old me gone away
Dead to self, alive to suffer
But neither is the ending there

I saw 'twas true that I was two
That in this new duality
As one suffers the other laughs
As one maddens the other strengthens

Feed the other to starve another
All it comes down to is the choice
Which me deserves the attention
To which do I give the voice?

Untitled

In my hand I hold a universe
And one is holding me
In turn
It goes like this beyond forever
And eternity

My eyes behold the future
In my microcosm seeing stone
I laugh and cry to see the fates
Of all those I have loved
And known

All the worlds inside of me
Are holding hands inside of you
Equations solved
Fly through my head
But I wonder why the sky is blue

What Escaped and What is Left

Dreamed a tree with liquid leaves
Growing in a place of knowledge
Surrounded by prisons of glass
Some empty
Some containing serpents
Asked the people seated near
None could give a suited answer
As to where the other snakes had gone
And why the caged were kept right there
This all took place within a mind
A mind which strives to know the meaning
And thinks perhaps the truth is closer
Than any comfort can allow

A Bright Dark Obsession

Now I had found you
In a place
With colored paper
Making origami cranes
Of blue and gray and green

You looked up and smiled
"How do you
Like my garden?"
I was very sad
But Why I didn't know

Till I saw I held a candle
Till I felt it
Slip away
And I saw the fire growing
You were all that was left

Now I have lost you
In a life
Because a nightmare
Becoming more when I awoke
Don't play with matches little girl

I've never felt older
Could not quite
Act my age
But the fire sings and
Changes more than I can alone

I followed every candle
Till I felt them
Slip away
I let the fire consume me
Till you were the only other thing

But the flames were so demanding
And I under
Their spell,
I listened to the singing
And now nothing is left at all.

Old Fashion Worm Hole

A splintered thought
A tattered paper
Shreds of an ancient life
Words that make it
New again
In the eyes
Of one young person
Words have wove
A bridge through time

Layers

Life is made of different layers
Many colors, strange numbers
All the things that we can see,
Just fractions of what can be
Gama rays and infrared
The lights we could see instead
Imagine if we could see all
Dream that there was no wall
Think of mysteries laid bare
What would we do, if they were not there?
If all equations were thus solved,
And no more could knowledge be evolved?
What kind of life would we then live?
With nothing more for us to give,
Would we not pray for catastrophe?
To free our minds from atrophy?
Thank God that this isn't true,
That there's yet more for us to do
Life is made of different layers
Many colors, strange numbers